YEARLINGS

Also By Frank Kearns

Circling Venice   2013

YEARLINGS

Frank Kearns

Los Nietos Press
Downey California 2015

Acknowledgements

I would like to gratefully acknowledge the editors of the following journals and anthologies in which these poems first appeared.

Cadence Collective: Long Beach Poets: "Honda 250," "Love and Relativity," "Outdoor Music," "Waiting To Cross Florence Avenue," "Walkway Maintenance," "Western Cooking," "Outdoor Music."

Lummox Poetry Anthology: "Insomnia."

Men's Heartbreak Anthology: "Words for Rain."

I would like to thank Carol Kearns, Lorine Parks and Patti Scruggs for their help in finalizing this collection.

For nearly five years I have had the privilege of working with the Second Sunday Poets: Margarita Escurra, Steve Gross, Lorine Parks, Zaida Ramos and Patti Scruggs. They have helped me with nearly all of these poems in one form or another.

Interior and Cover Design: Frank Kearns Author Photo: Carol Kearns

Second Edition

ISBN: 0692473351
ISBN-13:   978-0692473351

For John,
you are always on my mind

Table of Contents

Yearlings

we were running in the evening air
the top of the hill our finish line
both of us panting at the end
she so near to me I tingled
as a mist of breath caressed my cheek

this morning boys jog in the park
a tall girl swings on a low tree branch
yearlings   faces not yet marked
they feel the sunlight on their face
dampness of the still-wet grass

later we were together   close
in the deepest corner of the empty house
the scents of hair and skin and earth
all the many colors
                of the end
                        and the beginning

Mt. Katahdin

half way up an open slope
a lean-to by a narrow trail
where the legs of little boys
give up short of father's goal
and mother gathers us around
to sit and rest and eat

a creek is burbling far below
though its water is barely heard
above the ever changing wind
and here   an adult's minor pique
at the limits of our childhood feet
is surely not a matter of concern

a day in the sun
Hershey bars from mother's pack
yet after sixty years have passed
I still see father standing there
hands on hips   perhaps a smile
chocolate and salt
in my memory

Christmas: Orono 1956

We would sit on the bank and feel the tremble
of the southbound passenger train
as it rolled across the Pine Street grade

trailing a lone red signal light
that beckoned us south to Bangor Maine
down to New York and way out West

but for now we were grade school boys
Christmas pajamas and a model train
stopped on a flimsy oval of rails

all waiting on the vagaries
of electric circuits in a little house
taxed to the limit by the chill

of winter air against the cracks
fuses blowing at the demands
of Christmas lights and electric oven
glowing just above the tracks

Catholic in Orono

To be Catholic in Orono was
to live down on Broadway by the river
a long up-hill walk to Main Street

to be Catholic in Orono meant that
as you passed the porches of the those big houses
none of your friends would be there

to be Catholic in Orono was
to go to school in a gray stone building
in the shadow of St. Mary's church

where sixty students sat in rows
in the combined third and fourth grade room
a black veiled nun the only adult

being Catholic in Orono had nothing to do with
building igloos in a cold field of frozen snow
listening in bed to Sky King on the radio

or going barefoot all summer
in the thick grass nourished by
the mists of the Penobscot River

but it meant that Eddie Seward
whose dad owned the trucks that filled
the oil tanks of the houses in town

did not go to your church
and it was a mortal sin
to set foot in his

Dreams of Mother

It was not the sight of the
        peeling paper

on the farmhouse
        living room wall

nor the taste of the
        cucumber sandwich

with mayonnaise and
        slightly stale bread

not the clanking of
        dishes

nor the whir of
        refrigerator

and certainly not the distinct
        smell

of cigarettes that filled the
        house

it was not the sight of
        mother's face

love reflecting in every
        smile

but rather
        her touch

her hand
        on my shoulder

gentle
        almost tentative

that jolted me
        awake

Common Things

On our first morning in the house
our new home not yet cold
from its last abandonment

we tiptoed on our thin young legs
down to the cool cellar
heavy with the scent of stone and earth

we found a workbench with a few hand saws
tinged with rust in this electric age
and on the floor a 12 pound sledge

useless   with a splintered handle
that could have easily been replaced
if anyone had cared

half way down the basement was
a heavy timbered room
about ten feet on either side

with a door that barely yielded
to the pull of a ten
and an eight year old

but when it did and when we groped
to find the switch
a single hanging bulb lit up

to reveal a large square chest
a room within a room
a poultry incubator six feet tall

varnished oak with frame and panel doors
drawer after drawer of wire mesh
brass hinges and latches with long thick handles

handles that pulled easily
handles cast without a care
for a bit of extra metal

handles as long as a young boy's arm
with graceful curves to welcome the hand
and a thickening at the end

to signify nothing but the maker's sense
of how such a simple metal piece
should look to the eye and feel to the touch

good for nothing now except
to fasten closed a wooden door
if there was something left to seal inside

good for nothing but to teach
a little boy the feel of common things
and help him understand what beauty is

Basement Photographs

In the cellar
you   and I your older brother
construct another project

the trains of childhood
replaced with a model race car track
built by us from wood and foil

in the picture you and I
heads bowed in concentration
don't seem to feel the need to talk

but as we planned
the roadway slope
and the spacing of the track

we must have talked
and though I never was a dreamer
we must have talked of dreams

the photographs
are black and white
like shadows   like my memories

John

I don't remember words we said
as we climbed the slope behind our house
or walked the woods to the old dam
to see the icy water piled high

when I was still the older brother
and you were not the one who rode
his motorbike to Montreal
and returned to tell us stories
of old stone walls
and the sound of French
across a noisy bar

You told all that   and still
as I walk again to that little stream
I have spent a lifetime trying
to remember the sound of your voice

Haggetts Pond

All summer we'd row the heavy boat
to the nearer coves off to the north
catch buckets of sunfish and perch
or run aground and wade ashore
to sit beneath the old growth pines

but maybe once or twice a year –
I don't remember if we planned
to go out early with a bite to eat
or whether we just would decide
after a few pulls on the oars –

but maybe once or twice a year
we would point the bow across the pond
to two faint outlines on the opposite shore
and pull for what seemed like forever
pull against the rippling head-wind

trade off our seats a couple of times
till we rounded the two small islands
to linger off the half submerged rocks
or bob a worm by the sagging dock

what we never did was push the bow
into the pebbles of that pocket of beach
to splash through the water and finally step
up on the overhanging bank

enough in those days to get to the rocks
right at the edge of another place
so easy to enter   yet if we did
we felt that we could never row back

Ready to Go

The weathered barn
dusty bay in the far left corner
the nineteen twenty nine Essex

upright steel box of a body
yellow cracked wood-spoked wheels
the grease caked hard on the spindles

the upright bench seats
dusty seat covers somewhat worn
but still intact

the open glove box door
World War Two gas coupons
casually thrown inside

plenty of gas
for next week's trip to Boston

Heading Toward October

We all are heading toward October
buses   planes   and cruise ships even
going to see the October of
New Hampshire and Vermont

going to see the gold   the scarlet
the deepest shade of orange
and my favorite transparent yellow
glowing in the setting sun

after the bed and breakfast bustle
all day rides through folding hills
we plan to travel safely home
just before November comes

with naked trunks and twisted limbs
when all the deepest forest is revealed

§

Outdoor Music

Ghost Stories

The close sun of Los Angeles
is hard on ghosts
you won't find them as you might
lurking deep in redwood forests
or soaring on the wind
in the high sky of Mojave

In the light we tell our stories
cheerfully with bits of lunch
       at noisy restaurant tables
quickly in chance market meetings
or bravely in fluorescent
       story-telling classrooms

The ghosts prefer to hide and wait for dark
to float down moon-lit river channels
tiptoe among the black palm tree silhouettes
echo back the words they hear
       in corners of dim living rooms
collect the things that we have hidden deep
and then explode us from our deepest sleep

Seven A.M. Bus

Orange aluminum
dull gray windows
your high rubber tires
roll through the morning damp

you pump your pistons
lumber on your way
sweeping up the women
from the morning dark

they hold your cold seat rail
stare out the window
step down onto wide streets
enter large houses by the side door

tonight they will wait for your return
looking down the road
past the lines of cars
straining to see you in the dark

roll your tires
spew your smoke
work your swaying
orange magic

change them back
into mothers who
will tuck their children into bed
and hold their husbands' hands

set them free tonight
these women
of seven A.M.

Western Cooking

Her presentation finished
she stands before the group
jet black hair
dark business suit
light brown skin a hint of flush

In the pause   before the first question
the vision is back again
a stream of cold dawn mountain light
as grandpa cracks the hogan door
rifle in hand
in search of fox

Meetings over
stopped in evening traffic
cell phone blinking as her husband talks
the kids have choir practice
get some take-out on the way

Eyes on car in front
don't allow the memory
of rising mist
below the brick-red mountain
but most of all do not allow
the smell of fry bread
cooking on the open fire

Local Boy

He leaned back
arms by side
his shoulders straight
and sang.   He felt
the power of his voice
anchored by his
rock-like pose
his energy
his strains of joy
belting long strong notes
in front of the snappy
but rag-tag band
the joy of being
after all the drugs
the joy of singing
after not quite catching
the peak of the punk wave
the joy of living
after not achieving
the fame of 'X' or Patti Smith
the joy of friends to hug him
after decades in the dark
the joy of the
old time
ragtime
washboard rhythm song
the joy of the bass
the fiddle
and his voice
his own voice
soaring and alive

Walkway Maintenance

I'm on a rigid schedule tonight
no second beer no savoring another
hour-long episode of a popular police procedural

I have an early morning date
with a seven inch hand grinder
and a section of concrete walk
that has slowly lifted over the last five years

the ladies who come for our Sunday poetry workshops
are now in danger of tripping themselves
and the thought of the mail woman
in her rush across the lawn
causes me worry that cannot be ignored

the walk bends around the olive tree
old when we moved here thirty years ago
the walk is a relative newcomer and the tree
has made its displeasure known
by causing cracks that we let go until
a graceful section took a definite skyward tilt

so I'll get up early and rent the grinder
and bend over that corner for a couple of hours
if all goes well I'll have it leveled
before the heat gets too extreme
I'll return the grinder early enough
and only get charged for half a day

that should fix things for another thirty years
the olive tree is in no hurry

Las Palmitas

Limón, fresas, naranja juice
menu splashed with colorful cups
liquados, elotes, vegetable drinks

The sign says *5 Locations To Serve You*
The weathered face of a grandmother
smiles at the taste of a cool red drink

a six-year-old girl savors her ice cream
I remember dripping scoops of vanilla
from a rumbling freezer in a far away store

the grandmother says that her drink is *chamango*
mango mixed with a sauce called *chamoy*
first step   soak the fruit in salt water

till the nectar becomes infused in the brine
then mix in a bit of chili powder
while vinegar can be added for bite

bitter   but still
the taste of the fruit
lingers on the tip of the tongue

long ago I worked at McDonalds
chocolate vanilla and strawberry shakes
poured out from frozen 5 gallon bags

the grill filled with row after row of beef patties
ground and stamped in uniform circles
now I ponder the meaning of *tortas de pierna*

which she tells me is the leg of the pig
she twists her hands sharply to pantomime
the quick separation of limb from the carcass

and smiles as if to say *that's how it's done*
natural   practiced   the feel of the bone
right here on location to serve you

Outdoor Music

Scraps of conversation ripple
across the outdoor patio
like wavelets on a farmyard pond

every one a tiny gem
a rise and fall
a glint of magic

each ripple like a poem
a note plucked on a harp
most beautiful when it is lost

in a swelling sea of sound
or an expanse of sparkling light
spreading out across the avenue

Shelter

the sun beats hot in my part of town
the bus stop benches are bare metal gratings
on a narrow concrete sidewalk

there are other places not too far away
where an elderly woman with
clothes the somber colors of earth

can wait for the one eleven bus
with a bit of dignity
in the shade of an ornamented roof

in my part of town
the benches are inches away from the street
the sun beats down   and here and there

an old man stands by a stoplight pole
sideways in the thin gray shadow
searching for relief

Old Man on Slauson Avenue

I hired on 50 years ago
when the long gray sheds of Bethlehem Steel
filled the field past this chain link fence

off to the right on that sandy patch
electric furnaces clattered and roared
sulfur smoke rose and the steel boiled orange
with heat that scalded your face way out here

there on the left   you can just see the street
where the long rod finishing mill used to be
two dozen roll stands   three rollers apiece
turned by a thick web of drive shafts and gears

hot orange billets emerged short and slow
from a hulking gray furnace up at the west end
to be squeezed and forged through stand after stand

faster the hot metal laced back and fourth
rope-like extrusions the size of a finger
flying out onto the long cooling beds

it took hours of set-up for every new run
then Fernando and I and a dozen more men
would watch as the big motor started to turn

clank of the drive shafts
slow moan of gears
groan of the rollers
hiss of hot steel

there going into number four stand
as the steel began to pick up some speed
a spark and a flash as the tip hits the guide
and behind it loops of steel jumping free

in my dreams the hot orange loops fill the air
I stumble to find the emergency switch
as one curling circle envelopes Fernando
and pins him against the number six stand

in the daylight I come in this old pick-up truck
to feel my hand on the cold metal fence
to escape the nights when the clatter
and sigh of machinery
seem to take forever
to come to a stop

Lost (South East LA)

Ford Pico Rivera
GM South Gate
GM Van Nuys
Firestone Tire plant 1928
       the mocking skeleton still visible
       a *faux* Babylonian fort
       guarding the 5 Freeway

Bethlehem Steel
Slauson Avenue Maywood
Alcoa Aluminum
       rest in peace
              1926 to 1994

North American Rockwell
Kaiser Steel Fontana
whisps of corrosive dust in the air
and union jobs for everyone

Noon on the Rio Hondo

out on the wide spread of the West
the line between the earth and sky
seems so thin   and we so unprotected

here in the Rio Hondo wash
the sun teases out bits of mirage
from the hot bottom of the concrete channel

under the Montebello bluffs
a wooden roof and benches form
a place to hide from endless sky

a clump of men sit in the shade
some homeless   some have just come down
to pass the empty middle of the day

what to say about these men
who have no work to call them back
from the quick breath of a forty minute lunch

flap meat and onions sizzle
on a little grill
lunch preparations   but other than that

they meditate beneath their tree
on an airplane headed to LAX
and the march of sun down to the coast

while on a distant overpass
trucks and cars slow   then stop   then start again
radios play and air conditioners hum

and on this warm day when a beer will feel good
their friend approaches on a bike   a cool case of Modelo
balanced on his handlebars

Waiting to Cross Florence Avenue

The walk light at the end of the street
seems to take forever to come on
cars come down Florence quick and constant
flowing as an un-swimmable stream
of blurry colors and blinding chrome

a man on a rusty bicycle
sets his feet on the concrete walk
as plastic bags full of empty cans
sway back and forth on the handle bars

on the far side a woman in running shoes
leans against the stoplight pole
presses the metal button once
then pushes back in a long slow stretch

we have come to a stop at anywhere
like townspeople frozen on a page
of a yellowed hardbound picture book
waiting for the drawbridge to set down

sharing in casual nod and glance
this momentary intersection
like travelers bound together
by a pause on an ancient river bank
the ferry still at the opposite shore
the river moving fast in deep mid-stream

Paramount and Florence

I'm standing on the corner of Paramount and Florence waiting
to cross at the light. I'm thinking about poetry, and the magic
that I find in Robert Hass, and wondering what twists and turns
of imagination and real events led to a poem like *January*. I'm
thinking about how alone I felt in the park just a few blocks away,
by myself at a picnic table, in the shade of a tree, and how
even the school next door was silent with the children inside after
recess, and how the small birds picking at the nearby hedge
spend their whole life like this, under the sun, surrounded by
the colors of green.

And I'm wondering how a poet describes this urban intersection,
a field of asphalt baking in the sun; the way the cars flow through
and split off in smooth streams like the red blood cells flowing
endless through an artery. The subtle lean of the oncoming cars
as they sweep in an arc from the left turn lane, now heading right
at me before the steady hand below the driver's face maintains
the angle of the wheel, and the molecules of tire and asphalt keep
their anonymous separation as the car completes its quarter circle
passage three good steps in front of me. All this, and how alone
the electron is, how tiny and uncertain, and the emptiness
between its frenetic orbit and the nucleus of one vibrating
carbon atom caught in a tangled petroleum web that forms
the stage for this endless dance.

$\int$

Love & Relativity

Girona Twilight

In a small apartment in Spain
as the birds sing an end to the evening
my poetry seems like a game
while the life of the city is breathing

as the birds sing an end to the evening
voices float in from the terrace
while the life of the city is breathing
the sounds could be London or Paris

voices float in from the terrace
in the distance someone sings opera
the sounds could be London or Paris
I hear the sweet laugh of a father

in the distance someone sings opera
my poetry seems like a game
compared to the laugh of a father
in that small apartment in Spain

Orion

Strange feelings in my heart last night.
After stints and medication
we're in uncharted territory now.

Before the dawn
in the back yard with my dog
it's forty nine degrees

Capella shines bright overhead
and through a haze I see Orion
just as I expected.

Insomnia

This morning as I reached and pulled
our rumpled bed sheets straight
a book revealed itself as if
your secret lover through dark hours
startled half awake

Sometimes in the night I turn
to see your reading lamp so bright
a lighthouse on a rocky shore
or a probing lone searchlight

and here it is   a book about
Einstein as a youth in love
and I am frightened by
the wind-whipped waves
that roll on through your night

The Weight

The mist pressed silence on the morning
the way the heavy quilt
muffled the sound of the radio

just three nights before
we had heard a band perform *The Weight*
and this morning comes the chorus

drifting from your bathroom
not *The Band's* funereal march
but the soaring cries of Aretha

take a load off Fanny
and three women spread their harmonies
take a load for free

we had argued   you had said
the lyrics made no sense
and I said it's like a painting

the swelling voices like the rays
of sunshine just now finding
pathways through the morning fog

and as the hair dryer started behind the door
I felt your company all these years
holding me weightless and warm

Deep Space Neutrinos

It's a wonder of the human mind
that it creates a mathematics
to predict the most unexpected things
which then through exhaustive search
are proven to exist

Such is the neutrino
which turns out to be so small …
let's pause a minute to
remind ourselves about the atom,
the emptiness of it.   The vast distance
between the nucleus and the electrons
circling in their uncertain way
now matter, now wave …

still so much larger than
The neutrino
Small neutral one
able to glide through the atom's space
a constant barrage passing through
your hands, your fingers, face

Problems of Flight

Wilber Wright spoke
to the Western Society of Engineers
on the problem of flight as it stood
in the Fall of 1901

the importance of control

I'd like to talk to him about
       recent tendencies

the stall characteristics
       of the forward elevator

to drift sideways as I
       lean under the shower

the movement and reversal
       of the center of pressure

the problems of my flight
       still to be resolved

Love and Relativity

In the dark of the planetarium
I think about the rings of Saturn
and realize that when we lay together
I fit against the curve of your back

the way the third and fourth rings fit
close   but with a space in which
Einstein might have talked of love
as the transition of flesh into energy

or perhaps he meant the other way
because love for us is the oscillation
the transition from the fire of passion
to the feel of the earth when freshly tilled

between the melting of touch and sound
into a glowing orange heat
and the mundane placing of a picture
just above the living room couch

all of which is much more confusing
than Einstein's simple formulation

The Wedding Picture

It's only now
as I dust the glass once more
after they are six years gone
that the faces in the photograph
are not my mother and father
adults to the children
judges of our aspirations
but two young people
(in their wedding clothes)
looking off to the right at something
somewhere out of frame
looking for their life ahead
which lies there open and blank

Words for Rain

what name for a mist in early summer
that thickened on the canopy of pine
till droplets fell to darken and dapple
the paths which led around the pond
to the place we called Perch Cove

rain as verb   to lavish or bestow
great buckets of rain   so sudden
they absolve the layers of festering dust
that on a damp mid-summer night
break loose the clots of memory

what name for the driving lashing rain
that splattered on the windshield glass
in ever-changing circles and rivulets
and dodged the syncopated wipers
for one hundred turnpike miles

and what name will finally satisfy
the weeks of late September rain
cold against your upstairs window
disquieting the inner cracks
threatening to freeze and split the soul

Taking Apart the Tree House

I do it piece by piece
reversing the assembly

bending back each exposed nail
so no snag or injury

will come   I do it slow
I mean no harm

Bit by bit
each piece of well used wood

pries loose
an offering

to shadows and echoes
cycles of memory

bits to be hauled away

Honda 250

Raggedy little motorcycle
black and pitted chrome
bits of dirt and oil

tattered seat and
cables dangling just short
of catastrophe

good enough to putter
across Venice Boulevard
and over the canals

sorry enough to droop
its headlight in disgrace
at the sight of the big BMW

parked proudly on the grass
in front of your apartment
one warm Saturday afternoon

foolish enough to dump me
spinning on the tarmac
to the laughter of all the girls

just good enough to be
enshrined in our mythology
the golden coach

that carried us together
at the start of our
love story

NOTES

Mt. Katahdin: Located in Baxter State Park in central Maine, Mt. Katahdin (Elevation 5,270 feet) is the highest mountain in the state.

Catholic in Orono: The home of the University of Maine, Orono is a small town on the Penobscot River, about 40 miles from the Atlantic coast.

Haggetts Pond: A large pond (or small lake) in Andover, Massachusetts.

Basement Photographs, John: John Allen Kearns, January 7 1950 to November 27 1969.

Paramount and Florence: the poem *January* is by Robert Hass, *Human Wishes*, Ecco, 1990.

Old Man on Slauson Avenue: The 3300 block of Slauson Avenue, Vernon, CA was the site of the Bethlehem Steel plant from the 1950s to the mid 1980s. It is much different today.

Insomnia: The book referred to is *Einstein in Love: A Scientific Romance*, Dennis Overbye, Penguin Books, 2001.

The Weight: The song *The Weight*, by The Band (*The Weight* (single) and *Music From Big Pink* (album), Capital Records, 1968,) has been covered by countless artists including The Staple Singers and Aretha Franklin.

Problems of Flight: For an examination of the amazing engineering accomplishments of Wilber and Orville Wright, see *Visions of a Flying Machine: The Wright Brothers and the Process of Invention*, Peter Jakab, Smithsonian Books, 2014.

About
LOS NIETOS PRESS

Los Nietos Press is dedicated to the countless generations of people whose lives and labor created the world community that today spreads over the coastal floodplain known simply as Los Angeles.

We take our name from the Los Nietos Spanish land grant that was south and east of the downtown area. Our purpose is to serve local writers so they may share their words with many, in the form of tangible books that can be held and read and passed on. This written art form is one way we realize our common bonds and help each other discover what is meaningful in life.

LOS NIETOS PRESS
www.LosNietosPress.com
LosNietosPress@Gmail.com